PEN, PAPER AND POEMS

A COLLECTION OF 100 HANDWRITTEN POEMS

KANISHAA BARANEETHARAN

Made with ♥ on the Notion Press Platform
www.notionpress.com

To,

All my friends and loved ones.

my beloved, kith and kin.

Contents

Preface *xi*

Acknowledgements *xiii*

Prologue *xv*

1. A Cup Of Loneliness With Anxi-tea 1

10,000 Questions

Rage Rush

Tears Are Scars

People = Nightmares

Bloody Papers

A Fairytale

Infinity War

Be The One

Anger Is A Curse

OverthinKING

Emotional But Emotionless

A Hurting Truth

Remembering My Friend

Painting As A Colourblind

2. The Words Of A Love-giver 31

Red Tulips

From My Eyes

Confused Confession

Thursday Theory

Reciprocation Is The Medication

Contents

Gone Love

Before Leaving

Red String Of Fate

Cruel Reality

Angel's Favorite Draft

A Butterfly

L(ust)ove

Flames Of Hug

My Girl

Oh To Be Loved

Until Dead

Poetry And Polaroids

Nicknames

End Of Love

Lovetale

Title Of ___

Together

Throw A Book

Writing About Love

Wish?

A Saying

Notes

Vintage Letters

Love Over Distance

Contents

Lies

Adronitis

An University KID

To Repair Myself

Untold Or Unspoken

To Be Listened

Brown

Greed Or Yearns?

Lamp Post

Qualitative Love

Forever A Promise

Poetic Lies

Healing Therapy

Pretty Admiration

Stealing Your Prettiness

Dream Come True

Come To Me

Termed Goodbye

Coloured Charts

Unconditionally

Lost And Found

Birthday Wishes

Midnight Owl

Addiction

Contents

Half-Half

Sky Is Her Best Friend

Lyrics Of Love

Eye Contacts

The Yellow Dress

Pretty Eyes

Birthdays

For You

Hearts Entangled

Count Of My Love

Poerty Till Eternity

Let The Ditsance

Honey Eyes

Tour De Force

Kinfe Before

Metaphors And You

Nature Is Him

Best Friends Things

His Words On Me

The War For You

Their Beauty

A Worthy Line

Broken Beauty

Next Time Maybe

Contents

Letters For You

Butterfly Ring

To Live For You

The Grey Shade

December Till July

Fireflies And Boquets

Hope On You

Talkin To Whom?

Under The Stars

Preface

I'm a teen that loves to get lost in fiction and fantasy. Poetry is where my thoughts and words come in hand, writing has become my favorite part of my day leading me to a better world of poetry and literature. Writing of hearts that endured, love and so. I hope you enjoy reading all of the content I create. Take a look around; perhaps you'll discover what exhilarates you. Hope you'll like my works and support.

Acknowledgements

I would like to express my deepest gratitude to my friends for their unwavering support throughout this journey. To **daddypa and raji ma** who endured late nights and countless days on making me happy and work for my dream.

A special thanks to my best friends **Nivashini** and **Naathiga** for believing in me and championing it tirelessly. The editing team deserves an applause for their insightful feedback and dedication to shaping this book. Thanks to images from **freepik.com**

Finally, to the readers who embark on this adventure with me, thank you for giving these poem a home in your imagination.

Prologue

Hope you'll relate to some, hearty feel some, or atleast smile at some of my poems. Writing starts when a heart endures enough pain after believing the pen and papers won't "Break" you any more.

1. A cup of loneliness with anxi-tea

10,000 questions

I was wrapped around the

vincity of trauma,

nobody knew nor they realized.

Dead silence and suicidal thoughts

Conquered my end of fate.

Ten thousand questions and a billion

more questions marks hooked me up.

In the end, it's just me,myself and i

Against this tradegy of life.

Rage rush

I know you're vexed but rage and anger is Not always the solution,

Just a distraction or something mere Useless thing.

Not also the tears are a solution,

Speak your heart out to someone who Listens.

Anger is the emptiness fillingin you body.

A butterfly's burning wings will look Majestic while flying wild

But,who will know it's hurting the pretty Wilderness and help it?

Burning of rage is just hell's thing not an Angel's deeds.

Not even heavenly maidens will help you

Come across this hellfire.

It's only you can have control on, so think

Of it before lightning up fiery rage.

Tears are scars

I swear all pretty eyes will have tear burns.

It's just the lashes hiding it

And

The stubborn heart not wanting to pour it on others.

But,

Red eyes and swollen eyelids cannot be covered up.

Real eyes don't lie neither do they hide

What mouth refuses to say.

Tears burns are scars left from the

wounds in heart

People = Nightmares

if my tears were acid,I would be the ugliest person on earth.

If lonliness was gunshots,I would

Perhaps have a million of holes in my heart.

If betrayal were flowers,my garden looks like a desert.

If being loved was food,I'm for sure straving.

But, That's okay!

Because,

My love and care for you are pure like melody,

My efforts foe you are huge like mountains.

Yet, I'm the scariest nightmare people are afraid of.

No, people are my scariest nightmare!

Bloody papers

oh my, is it a curse to bleed on paper?

why would a lifeless pen and paper put life into my soul?

why not a real person?

maybe I should be happy that they don't judge and

talk trash about me.

I wish they could see how lively my notebook is

unlike the real me.

if I could I will fall into my own stories

I write in my notebooks and never come back.

this is what I call my therapy,

writing myself on

blood splashed vintage papers.

A fairytale

let go the fairytales,

find the reality that feels like a fairytale.

it's hard enough to test you but

easy enough to hunt it.

a man, woman or a thing.

oh human decency,

this is what we pray for,

prosper us with love and support

Infinity war

An infinity war without blood stained satin

provoked because regrets stabbed and caged my

heart.

maybe I was cursed with an infinity war that'll

neither be won nor given up.

an infinity war, an infinity curse.

Be the one

Be a butterfly lost in the woods, explore what's wrong and right.

Be the moon, learn to hold the darkness and stand alone.

Be the waves and tides, run and splash your love to your loved ones.

Be a flower, soft in personality and vibrant from the soul.

Be you, live your heart's full, become the beauty of

randomness

Anger is a curse

yes I am rude, arrogant and scary!

all the silly things you did hella irritated me,

you killed the lover girl in me that not even I can

bring back her,

I drank toxic tonics you served me thinking you gave

me a jar of honey nectar.

nah please don't act kind or even try to prove me

you're right, I know what you're!

what you've been and what you'll be!

shutting doors in darkness so no Medusa's snakes

come in, no devil's bat can knock.

OverthinKING

3 AM thoughts are not overthinking, they are the actual ones.

Because,failing in life is my biggest fear and

so does not succeeding.

my fear of imperfections and not being good at things are just

reality striking randomly.

efforts and hardwork haven't worked me enough.

maybe I'll fail? maybe not?

the deepest thoughts on darkest nights,

if death finds me,

may it find me alive stabbing myself

in the name of failure and

band-aiding in the name of success.

Emotional but Emotionless

I was the most chaotic, active, lively of all

but now, I'm somewhere lost between emotional and emotionless.

but why so?

random anxiety attacks and insecurities are popping up,

my eyes are burning, heart is getting heavier.

even little things are irritating me lately.

is this what depression feels like?

turning me into a dead meat? departed?

lifeless being?

only if I could escape from time, I will be relieved

and pull myself together once again.

A hurting truth

broken glass

shattered

on ground

will

cut bleed

your feet

even though

red roses

are bestrewed.

Remembering my friend

Would people's face just disappear from

the photographs once after they're no more?

To those lookin at it, our heart's aching the voice

of the corpsed is so pleasingly haunting for us.

The words, the talks from a distance so far made us laugh.

For you, the eyes are shedding tears.

Life is so unpredictable, but why so?

Now that you're no more,

We feel half the home in disrupted.

Half the heart burnt, Half the soul empty

people would remember you

Even If your face disappears from the photographs.

Painting as a colourblind

I wanted to paint

The town with

Colours, but then

Realised I was a

Colour blind

Standing with a

Grey pallet.

2. The Words of a Love-giver

Red tulips

Have you seen red tulips?

yes, the ones that's hold royalty in em.

being held in her pale hands and the vouge magazine

wrapped up made the tulips look elegant but,

my girl looks even more elegant.

when she wears her red and gold satin embroidered gown,

woman, she's the moment!

no fresh red tulips can beat her warm smile.

no vouge magazine covers can wrap up her beauty.

she's the metaphor for my red tulips

From my eyes

In the midst of

white daisies,

she was

the one

my eyes adored,

I'll never

be tired

of her beauty

and

elegance

nor will i let it lessen.

Confused confession

some debts are paid with pain and regret

but I would be graced to pay you with love,

once the moon is high up,will you take my hand?

Will you let me take out on a walk?

You're so beautiful!

My heart is refusing not to confess

But, I don't think I can go away without

confessing

Thursday theory

It hurts to core, but nothing can be changed, ain't it?

we shall meet the next thursday"

Thursday, midnight, signals is where we all fall in love.

authors and writers would definitely write

the next line was thursday.

only if the theories were so true, will you return to me so soon?

just like the next line of a book?

will you come to me with all the love you took away walking?

just like the main characters of the book?

thursdays and love is tied up together, me and you?

let's tie ourselves together the next thursday and fly high.

shall we?

Reciprocation is the medication

I do pour all my love on one person but don't I deserve it too?

Being so hurt that you cannot put your feelings together

to even express yourself is so bad.

if the artist cannot explain his paintings

then no one else can?

that's vain! so painful! don't drain yourself,

dreams and fantasy sometimes ditch you.

you breakdown for no reason

but it's not your fault, all you want is a little love.

you're longing for love to repair yourself

Gone love

bring back which once was mine but it never left,

glow, glam and glitter but shined in sadness

you were well intertwined with my soul that I was

able to forgive you for emptying me which

overwhelmed with light.

dead flowers are a sign of happiness in the past

which flourished the hallways of lifeless life.

hearts that endured and thoughts that gone through

are all just dawn and dusk, they'll perhaps come

again or maybe not leading to ends of everything.

Before leaving

5ft she was, his little girl holding chocolates, the huge smile

and warm hug complimenting eachother

one eye contact and

one head tilt, healed wounds, stitched cuts deep

down my heart.

until we meet the next time, may the hug I gave give you

comfort and warmth my heartbeat,

my muse my hands and yours may them wrap

around once again.

Red string of fate

will the red string pull us together? maybe or maybe not.

one fine day, let the angels above clouds,

glue us together without doubts,

I put my trust on folktales and destinies,

hoping they will not gift me adronitis,

when we meet, let our past memories rewind,

let the future untwine.

making me feel you're mine even before birth,

later death and afterlife too.

oh red string of love! will you? or will you not?

pull us together someday?

Cruel reality

My love story is too simple for the world being so complex.

Because, reality of this globe is that it's has standards

and be judged, leaving my teary wet eyeliner smudged.

only if I did care,

we would have happily lived in my vintage stories.

I cannot love you neither unlove you.

if someone ever read our story,

if the heavenly maidens hear it,

let them bring and bind us together for all 13 lives.

Angel's favorite draft

for once in a lifetime,

will i hold your hand till the end of time?

so as to feel what is love.

what did I owe to the angels to be blessed

and bound to fall in love with you.

perhaps, no wonder that all the falling stars,

4 petaled clovers,

all the dandelions I ever touch

already knew your name.

may our story be the angel's favorite draft,

so at the brink they pour their art craft.

Enter Caption

A butterfly

hands to a pink rose which had softer petals

than the shivering pale hands,

but chose to fly back and find love

in the garden kept lively by the hands of a little girl.

the midday's scorching sun an amber spotted

butterfly one broken wing tho,

about to die in heat found someone's pale palm

willing to save it.

leaving the cold smiled warmly and the pretty grasses

and flowers became a beautiful painting when the

butterfly flew.

L(ust)ove

so pure was her soul not so perfect but,

nothing else ditched people, but it.

none visualized the beauty in her like

she saw beauty in everything.

alone was she, the midnight moon and a bunch of flowers.

when the flower dies,

will the standards be erased?

and one will heal her trauma?

one heart! and one heartful soul!

amen, take her to where she belongs.

Let her rest in your utopia.

Flames of hug

she hugged him so tight that they have

to burn them together!

the pecks of flame rubbing onto the skin

just like their hug,

so warm and hot as fire but the last and

final, the wider the arms and fire spread the

more comfort and burnt marks,

the more red fire, the most the light

as like,

the more the closeness, the most the happiness

you're my falme hug

one, once and only

because, I would

My girl

you got the eyes, the smile and

everything you do just makes my day.

I will write about all the small details that lights up

the rest of world's paper and pen would cry

for not being held in my hands

that holds the softest palms of yours.

you're the drug that insanely

increases my dopamine and that makes me feel high.

intoxicated? yes, on you!

craving?yes, for your presence, for your attention.

addicted? yes, your beauty, your heart. put up a smile,

that just adds up prettiness to your beautiful face.

Oh to be loved

I write about love like,

I know it so well.

to be real,

me and love haven't met,

neither crossed paths.

how does it feel to be loved?

I only knew metaphors and similes.

Until dead

for till the earth collapses us into deadcorpse,

hold me tight, may our souls be tied up with the red string of fate.

be the poem I loved to write, also

will this poet be yours to love, too?

so divine that the book of our love

be praised like Bible.

let the maidens treasure our souls

in the heaven's garden.

Poetry and Polaroids

poetry trapped in a woman's body and

polaroids printed in a man's heart.

are bound to be washed away together and be

drowned in the sea of love.

the shore of memories being always wet and muddy

is their tides of care for each other's.

the last day when the earth dries up the poem

written on the back of the polaroid

will be buried into the sandcastle of love.

remembering their life and love never ended.

Nicknames

forget nicknames,

you made my name sound pretty.

everytime you call out my name I'll be like

"yeah that's me"

and a billion butterflies

fly around me.

End of love

how much did we love each other?

to define is to limit I answered.

pearls on his eyes burned in fury,

I lied and I buried the truth in jury,

only if I had guts to face whatever came crashing in

our world, in each other's,we would have whirled and twirled,

tonight our memories hit up like waves,

and I'm drowning in craves,

together we melted our waxed statue of love,

we saw it burning bright in people's agony and jealousy,

none of them knew our intimacy!

may the beloved tree of life,

give us our kingdom and thrones to lead a happy ending.

Lovetale

we were woven together in love not just it,

but also with care.

together we grew up to be tangled in each other's arms,

what made you let go off me and find another man?

not that you left me hurts me anymore,

but if we ended up together,

it would have been my lovetale written in a birdfeather,

the only thing I regret was not saying

how much I loved you, if I did you would have knew.

my dear, it's the actions we do for love,

nothing else below or above.

Title of ___

some people are poetry,

some are long essays,

some are rhythmic songs,

some are admired articles,

while me being a mere phrase.

what hurts is,

I'm never going to be someone's title for any of these.

Together

our souls

are

tied together

but

flesh and bones?

they've

been

pulled away

from

each other's

Throw a book

if you threw

a book at me,

I would

see ur doodles

and

sketches

and

have dried flowers

on the pages

that

have my favorite dates.

Writing about love

maybe I wasn't lucky enough

to fall in love

but,

I do know to admire falling in love.

and what I love even more is,

writing about it.

Wish?

I may not be the best writer/poet, but the best thing I

write is our story.

we're just a hundred and 73 miles away but feels like

we like in alternate galaxies.

my dear, you give me love more an I expect and even deserve.

I feel like I cannot express as much you do but I

swear I'm putting my fullest.

I may not be perfect but I am sure my soul

is generous and pure.

I am no God nor Almighty but I promise to protect You.

I am more than happy to be with you,

I just can't find anything better simply.

my dear.

A saying

it's better to be the poet

rather than being a poetry

when the lines we expect aren't best to be weaved.

remember,

not all the things that are written on vintage paper

are poetry.

Notes

O brawling love! O loving hate!

in the poem notes,

I spill my love the love I wanna spill on you.

maybe I should become less gushing in love,

else I have to find ways to bind with you soon,

you make me go crazy for your love and attention,

so when are we gonna actually fall in love?

vintage?modern? atleast in the afterlife?

when will you let me hold your hand?

Vintage letters

it's late 2000's

yet you adore the way i am still glued to

old times of love.

I loved writing vintage love letters, especially for you!

my handwriting and words are ancient poneglyph,

waiting to be thread-beaded by him.

you wanted to read my love poured words so,

I never stopped writing.

Love over distance

my heart is full of you,

I can barely call it mine anymore.

we are broken by distance yet, so filled in love and comfort.

I would love to be right next to you but,

miles and time are my only enemy.

why would destiny play so hard?

why doesn't it let me have you by your

arms? bringing back thoughts, my reality knocked,

the reality of us being apart.

at last, at least, will I end upon you?

a happy ending for me.

Lies

All the promises you made are pretty lies,

all my star drawn scars are

bleeding not because you stabbed it again but

I believed it wouldn't be you.

nevertheless it was my mistake.

if I wasn't the player then

I'm definitely getting played.

you are chaos personified for my peaceful scenery.

Adronitis

I'm afraid of not making you happy

with what I have because,

you say I deserve better but

I don't think I deserve any better than you.

you say you aren't enough for me but

am I even enough for you?

are you not wanting me to stay? or

am I making you feel worse?

I feel something from you, don't you?

if not so, I feel guilty for not making you feel so.

this shows I'm suffering from adronitis

An university KID

I was looking at my next door kid crying

with a snot in his nose saying 'mummy I don't

wanna go to school'

I was searching my little self in his face,

thoughts rewinding so does the smile on my face as a

17 yr old after applying for the university

the same evening,

school bus honked and I rushed out just to see him

running towards the front door with his oversized

backpack and a happy face.

I was smiling but isn't he the one that's happy?

maybe my memories collided and intertwined with his?

Enter Caption

To repair myself

I do pour all my love on one person but don't I

deserve it too?

Being so hurt that you cannot put your feelings

together to even express yourself is so bad.

if the artist cannot explain his paintings

then no one else can?

that's vain! so painful! don't drain yourself,

dreams and fantasy sometimes ditch you.

you breakdown for no reason but it's not your fault,

all you want is a little love. you're longing for love to

repair yourself.

Untold or Unspoken

never in my whole lifetime,

I want you but,

my heart never stopped loving you either.

you don't own me,

you never did tho,

I've neither feelings for confession nor regrets for not having so.

wishing I could erase you entirely from my thoughts and memories!

is this my kinda untold love

Or unspoken love?

To be listened

sometimes all we need is a heart to hear ours.

we want someone to let out our horrible or happy

moment till our soul is filled with nothing but emptiness.

flowers bloom and spread its scent

only so we can smell it,

just like we wanting our cherishing scent

to spread with our people.

waves hit up the shore so as it won't dry up,

however we are the shore wanting someone

to hear so we don't dry up even in our lowest.

so hear out people, they are wanting to be listened,

I bet they'll pour out what's inside,

every last drop.

Brown

if you were a shade you'd definitely be brown!

the way it soothes my soul can't be put into words,

your honey dipped almond eyes are view I embrace,

your tan skin upon me while you hug fills me up

with calmness.

the mocha coffee,

half sweet and salty cookies that

looks beaver brown are your palms and wrists

around mine.

It was my favorite colour.

Greed or Yearns?

The greed for reciprocation

or

the yearning for atleast bare minimum?

In the end I was just gifted with

"Nothingness".

Lamp post

the day my love died,

that night was dead silent not even the breeze was loud,

the lamp post's yellow light was always hurting our

eyes when we sit together that day,

it was the only thing that kept me warm and lively.

my eyes weren't hurting because of the strange

yellow light, but in tears.

I never wanted to stand beneath it, but that day, it

was my place to feel at ease.

thereafter, I didn't want to find another love, all I

did was cry under the strange yellow light lamp post

that gave me warmth.

qualitative love

if loving you was measured in quantities,

it would be,

as much as the Pacific Ocean drowns,

the sky expands and elongates,

from everest till Mariana,

the sun rays and moon light steeping grounds,

the emptiness filled in the galaxies,

and the number of stars in the whole universe.

that's how much love I've on you.

forever a promise

oh dear, I‘m here to love your imperfections and

insecurities, I’m here to pamper you and always fill

you up with love and energy.

but, I‘m afraid I won’t live till eternity to promise you

with a ’forever', also there is death to put an end.

but, till then if I hold your hand, I will shower you with

love and fondness. and embrace you with all that I can.

I would inhale my last breath in my death bed just

to say that I loved to till here.

Poetic lies

will o the wisp

his beauty can be deceptive I don't know but what if?

he liked me back?

maybe his look is pretty dangerous but, his words are lethal.

all these are just fables, false lies and fabrications in my mind.

"I hope he likes me back" is my favorite lie that I'll

let to ruin and devour me.

when I get lost in lies he'll be my false truth.

I am just a mere human but gifted with power to

handle fantasy like him. I am a poet and he is the poetic lies.

healing therapy

write me of love,

hope and hearts that endured.

the heavy soul of mine is filled with emotions.

your handwriting is my favorite kind of curved carves.

and your words put together are my healing therapy.

Pretty admiration

The moles and black dots of yours are stars falling

from the Multiverse.

the blooded bandaids are red lipstick kisses of your

loved one.

the scars and wounds are heavy rainy clouds with a

brilliant rainbow.

embrace everything you have, the prettiest

admiration results in pretty paintings.

Stealing your prettiness

the sunsets and sunrises stole your glow

to look so elegant while the honey

and flower nectar fought for the sweetness of your voice.

Also the soft grassroots took away

the scene of your wavy hair.

No wonder the red rose petals were the mild heart of yours.

white pearls grabbed the shine from your teeth

and yes of course the falling stars from

the galaxy beside are the specks sprinkled

in your eye.

Dream come true

staircases and stunning gown

all she dreamed of,

she made just hops on steps so euphoric,

that her man was lost in her elegance,

love admired the way he admired her,

and there begun the zing!

that lasted beyond eternity till infinity!

Come to me

He'll never be mine,

but I still long for our moments together,

holding hands, picking tiny flowers and so.

you know it actually hurts when you fell head over heels for him

but not able to express how you feel.

dear mine,

if you're not good at expressing love, come to me,

to experience what is love.

Termed goodbye

The moment I waved a goodbye,

even the door and doorbell was sad,

the cracked elevations and address board was

worried, the dancing trees and blooms felt grey,

stood there my loved one with a heavy heart racing

to stop me, I felt mine breaking into millions,

but the thought of us uniting once again put up

courage in me, my love, wait there,

I'm just ahead I promise to return with more love.

Coloured charts

spilling

colours

on a chart

is not art,

painting

life of

what

we love is.

Unconditionally

All I dreamed of is love,

someone that loved me unconditionally,

someone that loved me as if it's breathing,

but, they had other plans!

to look from outside, it didn't hurt nor painful,

the one that said loved me

scribbled in my soul as if an anxiety attacked

person's drawing.

for me love wasn't vibrant, also dark and grey,

in the end, it was a chaotic scribbled art.

loved yet unloved.

Lost and found

Get away from me!!

my mouth yelled aloud but,

my inner soul wanted to say:

in the labyrinth of life,

I found you like a sign board.

So, don't make me get lost again

the way I'm leading now is pitch dark

I hope you'll walk with me so that

rays of light shine on us.

Birthday wishes

My dear,As stars fall through the sky

Shine as bright as your smile,

I swear I would admire it till death My love

Your birth is something I cherish

Your birthday is something I would always

remember even for all 7 lives I live

So greatful I am to have you

Because people like you are very few

With the personality as vibrant as a rainbow

And a face so pretty thata prince would bow

May lord shower you happiness as rain

And love as snowfall.

Midnight owl

Past midnight like

the woods protect the owl

Oh, to be the one

he pulls out someone's soul

What's his is only his.

What's his is me!.

Addiction

My addiction

happens to be you

Oh,

to be heard

and

stared right into my soul.

Half-Half

Reciprocating feelings

is Never half-half,

one ofcourse overly pampers,

The feeling of our soul lighting up,

When eyes vision our loved one.

sky is her best friend

I bet the sky would be blushing pink

When you're around me,

with me,

standing close

She's my bestfriend talking to me through

The sun, moon and the stars

When you walk alongside me,

she be taking me to cloud 9 Through heaven

and back You and me.

Lyrics of love

You don't know how much I love this song,

You'll not be able to love this like

I do Lyrics of love

that I'll carve it on my heart

With a sharp compass.

Eye contacts

Just a

keen soft glaze

of his

Shattered me,

shooted my heart

In

love maybe?

Aren't I'm dreaming?.

The yellow dress

Golden Sun right after rise ,

Was the bright yellow colour she wore

Not handcrafted for her but chosen with love by her man

Among a pile of other 10 thousands,

He never knew it'd make her so happy.

A little kid had she became Shaking hips as if a 5 yr old,

The mirror might probably feel

Like my man admiring me. With love he gifted me that

I envy it with my whole heart.

Pretty eyes

Maybe my eyes are pretty but ,

My spectacles and hair prolly will hide it's Beauty

dumping my poor eyesight

When he tucked my hair behind my ears,

My eyes started right into his Vision clear

but blurred in blushing cheeks

Few minutes,few hours, Only till my eyeliner lasts

Only till my eyes aren't tired ,

It looks pretty but never missed to look what's

pretty and passionate

Him and his hands embraced

the touch of my face feeling till heart.

Birthdays

May today blossom for you,

With a lotta wishes and presents.

Let this year mentor you to be you

To love you, to build you,

May today make you happy and joyful

With my love so heartful,

Swearing none would show care upon

you Like I did, like my silly petty letters

and Flower do.

So Greatful was the moon to the sun

Not only for the light

also for the protection.

For you

For you,

my love

I'd

sacrifice

an ounce of blood.

Know that

I'll destroy myself,

Rather than

letting you go.

Hearts entangled

The sky's

bright and clear

Blue and white

intertwined

Prolly

inspired

by our oneness

Like

our

hearts entangled.

Count of my love

never did I know

There exists things beyond Earth

Only I knew,

I would find the bestest;

To present you and express my love.

The ground had millions of tiny stones,

That's the count of zeros after one

That my love towards you has.

Poerty till eternity

We are

nothing

but

Threads

of poetry,

weaved

Into

a tale of eternity.

Let the ditsance

Let the rain

Splash, ground

Split, clouds merge,

Thunders hit the

Distance between us.

Honey eyes

Your eyes in the

Dawn and dusk

Pours honey

That satiates my

Craving for you.

Tour de force

She was the

Pen and he

Was the paper,

Writing their own story,

But sadly there wasn't

Any reader to read that

"Tour De Force".

Kinfe before

Oh dear when I look at

You, the heart of mine

Embraces your presence

Even though you hold a

Knife against me.

Metaphors and you

Love is all about

How you metaphor,

Beautiful things like:

The smell of vanilla;

The sound of violin;

The touch of snowflake;

The view of mountain rage to your person.

Nature is him

She describes him as a

Golden cloud. As a deep

Sea, as a dark forest, as a

Humble breeze, as a stormy

Rain, all the wonders of

Nature is he himself.

best friends things

I was admiring her more than

She admires herself, I

Celebrate her success more

Than herself, I get angry

On others when they disappoint

Her more than herself.

I got her back,

Yes she is my best friend,

I do overcare about her.

His words on me

I asked him what

Does he like the most

In me and as he talk

Was lost in thoughts

Recreating myself the

Way he described me.

The war for you

What if all the

Mythical

Creatures team

Up and start a war?

I would standup all

Alone to protect you

Till the gate of heaven.

Their beauty

She

was

breathtakingly

Beautiful

And

he

was

heartthrobingly

Handsome.

A worthy line

It's just a worthy line of

Sentence,

in that paragraph,

in that page,

in that chapter,

in the whole book,

from the author,

which makes us fall in love with.

Broken beauty

sky has thunders,

fairies have broken wings,

roses have thorns,

diamonds have cuts,

skin has scars,

but that doesn't bring down t

he beauty of those.

Next time maybe

Like the poets say,

I'm made of memories,

He's half of my soul,

Not that I deserve,

But the best I'll ever have.

If not in this life,

Maybe the next with

all this life's finest memories.

Letters for you

Hope the letters

I don't post and notes you

hide from the host Be left untouched,

Cuz We never know

When our mind is not unhinged,

Of the standards said to be Cringed.

For us,

let the words appear to sight,

For the rest,

let it appear like pitch dark night.

Butterfly ring

May the ring

I wear shine upon your smile

everytime you think of me,

May the heart of mine feel warm

everytime you think of me,

May I never forget your voice and touch,

On the black butterfly,

I promise to cherish you

till the gates above the clouds.

To live for you

Life wouldn't have been so much good

If I haven't met you, maybe it was my fate

My heart wouldn't stop beating for you.

You turned an unwilling skin and bones to live

TO LIVE FOR YOU.

Bloomed my soul, drowned me in happiness

To have you in my life, maybe I haven't sinned, For

me to be blessed with your presence.

Thank you for making me a better person

By heart, you made me love life

So I'd live to love you.

The grey shade

The world is grey and wan,

Nobody's favourite colour was grey

But was her's with a heart so full

Of emptiness and of nothingness

Grey like the ashes, grey like the smoke from a cigarette,

people wouldn't care of grey

For once hurting to burn to inhaling death in lungs

For her beauty in grey was the moonlight

So fond of its lovers with a pale brightness

As hard as grey steel was her heart, non brittle

Why wasn't grey the colour of prosperity?

Wishing people would seek beauty in flowers hiding behind
grey rocks

Thunders from a rainy cloud Take just a glimpse on grey,

In an 'odd'inary way.

december till july

18/12 was someday Until the sun and moon eclipsed

I wouldn't have known it was her birthday.

The Stars falling for me to wish for her

The clouds hugged each other, Throwing thunder and lightening

Like love upon the earth. All the disastrous beauty is she herself.

She was the Chaos, so did she think But not as it is, she's my muse.

My love, may today be calm and peaceful

For you I would silence the entire universe

To say that I love you more than anyone

Niva! May the universe present you

A serene journey of life with success at the end.

Instead of mess and chaos all around.

Fireflies and boquets

Flowers growing in heart,wish i could rip em out

and gift a boquet of unsaid "i love you's"

A milion fireflies bottled up and

that's the light you give off

to the half blind eyes of mine.

Hope on you

Your eyes could swallow stars and dust

But,

What made me have hope of loving you?

Like the energy from the bigbang,

Endless and never worn off.

Even if the gate of death finds me,

Atleast i won't regret not trying.

But will be entering heaven

Empty and hollow

Without you my love.

Talkin to whom?

to bind into each other eyes

is she died for,

made words, scripted scenarios.

cold as ice yet

scorchig from inside

dead outside, alive in.

only for words to spillout.

Under the stars

Let us sit under the stars at pitch dark night.

talking our heart ou under the same sky.

all about how fear, flaws and fallacy

turned into love, laugh and life.

Each planet representing vibrant shades,

Lilac,emarald, orange, aquamaraine and white.

All encircling us,

shining so bright of great view for us.

I'd spill out my untold feelings.

Oh to sit under the stars with you,

makes me feel better by soul.

THE END

www.ingramcontent.com/pod-product-compliance
Lightning Source LLC
La Vergne TN
LVHW041203150826
845673LV00001B/273

* 9 7 9 8 8 9 7 2 4 1 8 8 0 *